ALSO BY BRENDA COULTAS

The Tatters (2014)
The Marvelous Bones of Time (2007)
A Handmade Museum (2003)
Early Films (1996)

THE WRITING OF AN HOUR

The
Writing
of an Hour

BRENDA COULTAS

Wesleyan University Press ~ Middletown, Connecticut

Wesleyan University Press

Middletown CT 06459

www.wesleyan.edu/wespress

2022 © Brenda Coultas

All rights reserved

Manufactured in the United States of America

Designed and Typeset in Whitman by Eric M. Brooks

Library of Congress Cataloging-in-Publication Data
available upon request

Hardcover ISBN: 978-0-8195-8070-2

Paperback ISBN: 978-0-8195-8071-9

Ebook ISBN: 978-0-8195-8072-6

5 4 3 2 1

CONTENTS

I

The Writing *of an* Hour

Hour I

The domestic dust of an hour: when a granddaddy longlegs has spun, from corner to corner, a network of webs and eggs.

Low radio bleed-through, partner walking and scraping something like dried egg off a plate, an hour after breakfast, and the hour before in the bath, the laptop by the tub but out of reach of the splatter, or is it better to say, the displacement of water, the waves a body makes as it enters another body and laps over the edge? I should learn something during bath time, so I listen to a talk on Peruvian ruins and their effects on local economies, the speaker says, "like village women selling while preserving traditional crafts." TED Talks on auto play, learning as I soak and after drying off, I could pass an exit exam.

Change the station, drying my hand and arm, and shutting the lid to be with my own thoughts about how to reduce cleverness in writing, to consider an assignment of describing lost sounds, like all the sounds in "Crossing Brooklyn Ferry," but mostly how to overcome writer's block, and how to do two things at once exceptionally well, and think I'd like to drop acid.

Heating soup in the kitchen, even though this is the hour of writing, glance at three French baguettes that need to be tossed into the woods for animals to eat: back on the bed, propped up and keyboarding, sniffles, and looking at blue socks on my feet, and this view of green grass despite the season, leaves of curled brown like butcher's paper and summer lawn chairs, and what about that humpback whale videoed in Hudson River, a singular traveler, through heavy boat traffic and if the whale is lost or sick, how lonely or not, is this mammal, who must surface to breathe.

Hour II

This is the hour of writing, raining and dark days of winter. Of
colds and crap, of umbrellas and hate when the wind blows them
ribs out. My husband follows me from room to room. And I wonder
if my domestic dust is more like "The Story of an Hour" or more
like "The Yellow Wallpaper"?

I cannot distinguish fact from fiction.
Houses from accessories
Bowls from pitchers
Armoires from wardrobes
Carriages from shopping carts

I steal into the ceramic shop to eat from white plates as thin as
saltines, some cabbage-shaped dishes and lobster-handled platters
that the British are so proud of. I carve houses out of a roadside bank
of clay, garages and arches court the danger of collapse and they do
collapse on the best matchbox cars, including sports cars with suicide
doors––and when I am the little match girl, I obsess over haunted
houses as much as Shirley Jackson, and I draw you into a warren
of rooms.

When I return from the hour, Mrs. Mallard is dead, and my partner
stoned and cooking and listening to a podcast of *Don Quixote*, and we
both are thinking of the Americas.

The Mending Hour

I tied one on, I mean I took my grandmother's apron, its strings
and glittery rickrack and I wore it on the streets of the East Village.
The apron is a cloak of superpowers, a psychic umbrella. I paraded
past Emma Goldman's East 10th Street address, and rang her doorbell
for a sip of water. My domestic armor is made of gingham even
though a woman is still considered an unelectable candidate.

An After Hour

When one thing is becoming another, when writing is morphing, when the writing of an hour becomes the desire to write at all hours and into the night, fueled on caffeine or wine and desiring instruments of writing; typewriters, even a nib and inkwell, and considering all the ways of stretching a space, digital or hard copy; hard copy, an ugly expression for printed matter, and for that matter, printed matter is efficient but lacks beauty. Page, a soft and elongated word; page, an extension at the end of my fingers; page, a screen that holds dreams and desires; the page of a legal document that binds. The page is a promise. I read all sides, turning the page counterclockwise and turning the page over for what I may have missed.

An Hour Earlier

Desire is a stick for scratching words into the dirt and for chiseling stone until the words become solid. The pen is a body, an anatomy, not an earthworm with indecipherable ends; the pen has a head and tail, and inky guts. And the brain of the pen belongs to the maker of marks.

A Late Hour

All the elements of the hour surround my laptop, in the dying blades of cut grass and in the dying battery. Finches continue their making of a nest of twigs and grasses, but I know the nest is early paper, the raw ingredients and pulp. I know the world is a page-turner, a paper globe, and I know that the birds are the great writers of the sky.

What I Fed the Hour

Envy and anger, and analogies of how one thing is and is not like
the others. I fed it glowing wire filaments from inside an Edison bulb.
I fed it the blue ink of blood by the shovelful.

What is happening in this hour? Neighbors moving out of their house,
flowers reaching towards the light, insects hovering, a puddle of water
fading in the sun and I read a long poem. Begin to consider the year
I might die of old age. And wonder if I will live to 2050, which seems
like a great long time from now. Hear the noise of the bathers from
swimming hole and I hear him grab his bong from the back porch.

A house cat forages scraps from the compost. I wish it was a puma,
a mountain lion in the backyard, chewing blades of grass. Admonish
self to address the material (page) instead of raiding the fridge;
dandelions (not mountain lions) thrive outside, and there are so
many that I will have to eat them.

Beginning of An Hour

The hour begins at 8:50 p.m. in my childhood room reading
A Handbook of Disappointed Fate by Anne Boyer. A podcast on
gender and chromosomes plays.

Earlier run to place small American flags on family graves. Walked
through tall weeds into my uncle's dream house. Dream for him
anyway, must have drawn the blueprints on a napkin. No sidewalk.
He never made one. The house looks like a sea captain's house with
a widow's walk even though it's thousands of miles from either coast.
Waterlogged and sinking, it should be bulldozed.

In this hour, came the year of asking for what I want. So I asked for
a year off work, I asked for writing space, I asked for travel funds, and
they all came. I gave myself permission to fail and to say anything on
the page and after all my loud self-talk, I fell silent.

An Hour of What I Still Do

My mother is a solid piano, she may be mahogany, she might be a
dogwood, with Christ-like wounds in the center of a white flower. My
matriarch is grand and made of black and white keys. My mother is
strings and vibration. Foot pedals and varnish.

I am over sixty
I have a mother
I am not an orphan
I always hoped that she would be with me for this long
I have a mother
I am over sixty
I am a child
I am her child
I am not free
I have three sisters and a brother
We will be survivors
I have a mother still living
My father is not living
I am not an orphan
Yet, her brother lived to age ninety-nine
I try to forgive her
I have a mother
I am over sixty
I will survive her

An Hourglass Running Fast

An hour of returning sweaters to drawers, of hanging blouses and of listening to thudding wet clothes going in circles, agitated. Isn't that the appropriate word? You have to agitate the clothes.

I stand by the spin cycle and I hear my partner's phone ping.

Small farm table behind me, red legs and soft pine top. Looking at books in the morning. The seal of the day torn off. Turn off devices to quiet the mind. I hate writing through the gauntlet. If I am away from writing for long, the voices reform and say, "there are better uses of time than making poems."

Straw handbag in red and white that I brought 100 miles north. Pocketbook from a poet, silks and soft garments. And another poet gave me orange slippers from China, plastic slides on wooden painted soles. I think of the givers and receivers, I know the provenance of garments and objects in my writing room.

Dump out a plastic bag of early writings, all pasted together and pressed in folds, an accordion. I read the accordion as a map and maybe there is a sentence that could be the root of something larger and greener. The accordion of raw thought, of raw art. I write "You Can Do It" in childish print. Pen mark of hesitation midway through and I tape a recused rift at eye level:

I didn't come out for the stars
Meant to but too lazy to put on shoes. [hesitation period] and a jacket
And I know they will show up
As [handwritten correction] luminous lava [handwritten period inserted].

Glimpses strong enough for carrying on, yet barely make it to the end of writing hour. Here I am facing a screen, shoes in hand, thinking of dinner.

The Hour of Making

The writing this morning begins with erasure. I delete the false starts, change gears, gaze beyond the screen and onto objects on the desk and back.

Everything is closed and I am bored with the restraints of masks, of cooking, of tv and podcasts. All the ways of filling space that people once filled. Inside my shelter, at the germy keyboard, a random sentence hour ensues from a bag of fragments and I wonder if I can ever lengthen these bits of thread.

Dried beetles
Octagonal skylight
Lobotomy needle / Nudity concealed by flyleaf / Blue glow working up nerve or heat?
Flintlocks, burnt buttons, buckles and coins
Garden petals in repose
In space the black void burst with color
Buried here, in this room under a pile, mummified with wild hair and parchment skin, skin that turns to paper. Or what is written on the face.

Riddles saved for later. I want to see "living room furniture in a ditch." And I mourn the tragedy of "The grandest house in a small town."

Hard Clock Hour

Flashback of factory clock: the punch in and punch out. Waiting
for ticks of the minute hand. The boss calls you into the office,
admonishes you for standing by clock or for low production, you
stamped out 600 parts an hour, 200 parts short. Did you come back
drunk from lunch and operate heavy machinery?

Did I get drunk instead of logging time at keyboard?
Neaten my nails to write, neaten my clothes, straighten shoes,
roll up rug.

Season the beans, season the room, the desk lamp, the line of pens,
the tangle of paper clips, and the lion's breath seasons the broth. I put
my face on and begin to write. The lion's fallen hairs become felt and
make a useful hat. The lion's paws warm my shoulders like a weighted
blanket and the lion's snore a lullaby. The purr of the lion's pleasure
pleases me. The lion has its own room and its own meat. It wears a
red coat in cold rain and greets me at the door. Nudges, rubbing nose
against my human legs. A truce between us. We had come to accept
each other, both locked inside a pleasant enough house, but we want
out. And we push at the cracks, push at the trap, like the little mouse
who made itself even littler, who banged and banged against metal
and squeezed out in reverse, fled the trap of the unknown with only
its nose for a guide, the nose that led it into the trap. Trap of kindness.

The Growing Hour

At night, arms crossed over chest. Or hands to cradle of pelvis.
Or palms cupping the outside of thighs.

A core of lettuce inside my water glass grows small spears of green
and a red potato sprouts tiny knobs. Moonflower seed in the dirt;
florescent green head erupts from its hard shell.

Inside of the hour, small shoots of plant life ask for a home in earth. I
answer the shoots and knobs with tender talk and with soft intentions
to grow a garden from kitchen scraps, and soon I will take a leaf and
I will eat. Meanwhile, I want to be caught writing, I tell my partner,
I tell my friends, I am going to my desk to write. And when I die, will
it be inside the act of writing? The occurrences within an hour, the
gamut, the beginnings of composition, of finding my face, my feet and
fingers. Situated, at a desk, the complexity it took to get here, to find a
surface, to write within plaster and aluminum siding.

Composing is a house of windows. Hundreds of rooms; each room
is a theater, an aquarium, a glass showcase; the interior remains
mysterious and window is the Norse word for *the wind's eye*.

II

A Channel *of* Soft Earth

HOUSES

I woke up and saw that my hands had become small chairs. I sat on them and fractured the left and the right. My hands were small chairs, I painted them in rainbow colors. Imagine this, after dinner my hands became tables. I placed several art books upon them and then a gooosenecked reading lamp. My eyes became eggs and fit comfortably inside my sockets; my sockets could have been egg cartons for all that it mattered. My tables became houses and we, my partner and I, moved in.

NIGHT SHADES

I

I asked for a book of wax; it was golden and thick, but it couldn't
be opened and couldn't be held even with cotton gloves on and it
couldn't be read near open fire or on hot days. Like Times Square,
it was astonishing to behold. I loved my golden book and so did my
friends who came to admire its radiant glow inside an archival box.
My golden book could not be shared with children at bedtime, or with
the bereaved needing comfort, or the confused needing wisdom, and
yet even as its brilliance blinded one's eyes, it remained beloved.

II

I went to a city of fishes and a city of witches and there I beheld the
red wool of a redcoat and I beheld the grand homes of sea captains
and a poet's library, and I beheld a judge's gavel and I beheld pewter
tankards and draughts of beer served in dragon-stemmed goblets,
and I beheld a shop that sold witch balls, a kind of glass sphere, that
caught the sun's eye, and dreamcatchers made of string and feathers
for rearview mirrors, rune stones and crystals sold in small dark
sacks, and I beheld a suite of tarot cards spread in a shop window and
bundles of dried and fragrant herbs hanging from ceilings, I beheld
spells for love and fortune cast from used paperbacks of the occult.

NOTES FOR A TEA

Take them a cake or fruit on a stick. I eat out of the jar and scrape the
skin of an orange and take my time to read handwritten notes posted
on the wall. Be kind, they said, sticking their signs in the lawn. Be
nice or leave, said the bartender, and I spit on all the paper napkins,
but I am always kind to the cashier

In the woods, I built an altar, not like in church, more like in nature
or in head shop. I carefully place rolling papers and a glass pipe in
harmony. There are teas for sleeping and some tea will bring you
wealth. Would you drink a tea for true love? Do you like or make
potions? I collect bits of paper, cast rune stones, read cards, and lay
out my best silk

To my love and to my beloveds, be kind and be akin, be righteous,
be soft and be firm, be pleased with yourself. Inside of our kindness,
which we wore as garments,
as in tunics, not jumpers or dresses,
our cups overflow with coins
our love invented an
animal

MOMENTARILY

"We are being held here momentarily"
said the conductor
on an island off the coast of Manhattan
by the silhouette of an asylum
where they make skeleton keys
out of rainbows and out of actual skeletons
from the catacombs of the Marble Cemetery
where people become Greek marbles
like a game of statues
industrial green
umbrellas are made here
rib by rib
and shoes
this an island of cobblers of Roman sandals
and we are held here monetarily, momentarily
mortality

CLOUD BREAK SONNET

Because there were clouds breaking over the moon,
I am trying to remember an earth science grade-school class
(after earlier Family drama overlay)
On gravity's pull and of werewolves and how
Blood must be made of salt water for the moon
To bring out the beast
A walk ensued inside of my mind
Stationary like an exercise bike, but that is a ride
Unless I am walking it to an air pump
Rain is falling beyond the disco party lights on the bed frame
Onto a pine tree of sorts and its needles absorb the hum of the fridge
I am not plowing through space
With a blue jay looking for scraps
Of compost, not yet turned
tailbone

WISHES

Shaker without the celibacy
Wired but off the grid
Amish without the puppy mills
Slow but with lightning wit
Veteran without military service
Captain of land and sea

THE COILS

I paid a visit to my vessel, made of clay, unfired, and waiting inside a bag
I gave it a dip of water

The weather was humid and sunny, but elsewhere snow
And the clouds, we took personally

We decide to sit on the shelf for a while
To reconsider our shape and purpose

I prefer that the pot had none
That we exist for mutual pleasure

Making a pot is like kneading bread. We run clay through a ringer
and how dangerous to get your hand caught. I am really going to
town now. Rolling out ropes of clay and building walls and using a
wooden wedge to smooth the coils into a charming pencil holder. I
am cooking now with my coil pot; we are talking about UFOs, of how
dirty the potter's wheel is, and how we are learning to throw pots
from YouTube videos. We need more water and we argue over what
is and is not a painting. We decide to keep on loving and to wash our
hands up to our elbows.

UN-WRITTEN

Not a fiction, although
I have told some tall tales

Not an essay
for I have no argument

Not a memoir
for I have already said it all

Not a suicide note
for I wish to live

Not a farewell message
for this is not goodbye

Not a message in a bottle
for I am not lost at sea

Not a poem
for I am out of beauty . . . .

Not a to-do list
for I am kept awake by all that I have left undone & unsaid

I took in particles through spiked nose
droplets of narrative
ran down back of throat

        & flooded

guts

                with a ponderous ark

& with a lion's paw in lap

                I turn off news & undo

In the bronzed chair
On edge of jungle and beach

I ponder the ark and flood
Hippos, sheep, and giraffes, two by two

Consider the manatee
As a snout rises up for air

How many days in close quarters?
Did Noah smell like

Horse sweat or hay?
More than one flood made this world

I ponder enormously
How wicked we were when the earth shook us off

SOFT EARTH MAKINGS

Humans cover the soft earth with nest making

weeds and trucks

hoods popped after an addict's rampage

tires sunk   partially buried

informal earthworks

Bathing and thinking of what the earth chooses to absorb

And what systems hide

Half in water   up to shoulders

Cavities in back teeth   among bits of mercury

Once in a boiler room of an elementary school and the janitor's closet

I bury under

Catfish fiddlers,
VFW (Veterans of Foreign Wars) dance halls
Turkey shoots
Tip boards
Bingo sheets inked to the table

                                                      ruts where the shed was,
        and other decay

        before HAULED out to visit the
                                        Relations

        What did the shed do but stand as a sentry of time

                                        for housing farm things?

POPPIES

Deer linger
in the cold
behind the surveyor's
orange ribbon and
the jumpsuit
they gave you
in the county jail
forces an image
into this poem
beyond winter
the fence between
us and the new
neighbors is made
of fallen trees

CATCH A WOLF

I take a book
in hand and
want to sleep
I belong
to the daylight
and to the smallest
of woodpeckers which during mating season make the largest racket
drilling
into dead oaks
I belong to a family of tiny noisemakers
it took more
than a year to quiet my mind
to be a beast of daylight rather than a nocturnal (drunken)
animal
I became
a daylight
beast
of
spiral notebooks
of bitten down
pencils
of stray
fur
shed
in
the
wake

SERVETTA MUTA

A body in Venice, of water or flesh or other corporal matter

To be a body in Venice, say Ezra Pound's body, surrounded by fir trees on San Michele

To be a body in Venice, pounding over the Rialto bridge to arcades of glass horses and gondolier caps

To be a body in Venice, eternally lying under glass in the nave of a chapel

To be the body, the body thieves stole, whose bones, hair and clothing are quartered and divided

To be the head of Saint Lucy, with her plate of eyeballs, the long stalks dangling and wet

To be the one who plucks the beards from the dead monks and who makes the effigies in wax

To be the ones who pull out their own teeth to make the Christ's teeth

To be pillars of bone sunk into clay

To be the foundation of paperweights and opera houses

To be a body in Venice engaged to the sea

To be a glorious and tawdry tourist

To be a body in Venice

MERCY

Body weight against wood
I have come upon a door and pushed
with all my might into a cascade of
splinters and worms

PLAGUE MASK

I will die on the *vaporetto* in the heat of August. I will die quietly,
behind the plague doctor's mask with its long nose of leather, stuffed
with a bouquet of herbs to combat death's spell

I'll die in a *vaporetto* on a minor canal. Maybe I'll die on a garbage
boat or be hand-carted to the lagoon. I will die crossing the canal on a
packed *traghetto* or tied to the timbers of the Doge's Palace

I will die in the heat under a lion's head in a fool's mask.
I will die in August when the grand beggars of Venice crawl face
down with palms outstretched

Everyone reminds me to read *Death in Venice*.
They remind me of why I died in August on the *vaporetto* in my seat,
behind the fanning, ever-elegant matriarchs of the Grand Canal

I died for Lord Byron
Died for all the love affairs
Died for green aqua light

I HAVE FORGOTTEN WHAT OTHERS SEE

My scar has a face that others see
A face that walks ahead of me
A rupture in the bark of a tree

To a future I cannot foresee
I own my wounds to a degree
My scar has a face that others see

Although invisible to me
The rough badges I decree
A rupture in the bark of a tree

Each scar sings a song
Splinters of summer wrongs
My scar has a face that others see

Of sweet babes and losses
Deceit and double crosses
A rupture in the bark of a tree

Beneath the frost
Wounds exact a cost
My scar has a face that others see
A rupture in the bark of a tree

ARCADES OF MIDTOWN

Sample sales inside lead paint hallways & buttons
boning & kente cloth
ostrich feathers & knitwear workers
en masse & hard to walk & difficult to eat & to be naked in the arcades

KNOT

My hands were not always autumn
not the oak or maple's veiny maps
My arms were not always perches
for migrating and imaginary birds
this waist wasn't always ringed with
thick and thin years and these feet were not
always roots drinking from the water below

CERTAINLY, THIS IS WHAT I WANT

Certain things
are some things
are the same
sometimes not
the dearth
is too great
sometimes it's
over there
behind
traffic cones
and melts before
the sequence
of naked wants
of fools
of good folk
of clean notebook pages
and tulips are good too
as they open
their faces
bend down
to cup
the earth

III

Journal
of Places

JOURNAL OF PLACES

~ August 4–5, 2015
Hudson Valley, Southern Indiana

A day of abandonment. I abandon the page, I abandon the summer,
the sun, the hammock: regrets as plentiful as grains of rice spill on
the countertop.

Reading Unica Zürn and thinking of *The House of Illnesses*, her
architecture. Wondering if I have the courage to feel the edges of
my practice.

Yesterday, ate like a mad woman. Buttery grilled cheese. Potato with
sour cream, burger, two beers. Mad cow eating . . . Long fast then
devouring fat and sugar. My fear of having everything and nothing to
say. At mid-life never to live in the abode above, my glance is at earth
level on the earth plain.

Yesterday, unveiling of a Sojourner Truth marker on Route 9.
A historian said, "This is the path, this is the tavern site, and this is
the house of refuge."

Dusk. After a swim. Microwaved a bowl of mud from the Dead Sea.

The path was square and Mom's clothes made an island in the middle.
What would you name that island anchored in the brown carpet? The
mainland consisted of more clothes, papers (stuffed into bags after
clearing the kitchen table), office equipment and a TV with VHS slot.
Still the old door, with a glass window and with ringer bell that made
a satisfying *briiiiing* as it turned, was blocked. Manual trill. Not the
short self-satisfied quip of a car lock.

A fantasy of building a cabin just for the pleasure of opening the
doors I love. All with original glass (almost wavy) Grandmother's face
emerging out of the dark to open the door. She unlocks it, laughs, and
I come in to spend the night. I slept in my grandfather's bed on the
other side and she liked to say, "Let's pull the covers up over our heads
and pretend like we're dead."

It was not a dream, there were old doors leaning on the trees.
I opened a thick one, like the door to a hacienda. Rough, tall and
majestic. Wormholes.

An octopus fills its lair with bits of curiosities making a cabinet in the
sea. It must be loaded with plastic water bottles and six-pack rings,
and maybe some Happy Meal toys: french fries with legs, palm sized
Batmobiles. Does the octopus save for a rainy day?

Two days after clearing the room of my father's twin metal bed,
a sibling began filling it with magazines and books (not literature
which never expires) but career and software manuals from the
last century.

The hoard is anger submerged. Human stash of malted milk balls in a
milk carton. Cleared a path to the dryer and found a leak.

Bed surrounded with coffee cups. Empty plates, even though she rarely eats. She takes the plate you made her and retreats as swiftly as the carved bird inside a German cuckoo clock. She returns to the painted bird's cloistered room, narrow and of plastic or wood: her exits determined by a chain and spindle cast as pine cones.

Underground chambers
As loquacious as headstones
Crayfish-built rooms in the mud
Correction tape stored in its original plastic bed
Will the bells ring or coins drop into the dirt?
Hadn't thought of my brain as a bell
Ringing it does
Heralding one in and out of the doors
I wear a bell as a warning and place a key inside that could unlock a
Book of Hours, and my name could mean black soil or someone who
breaks young horses.

Every night in my dreams, I blew up the high school, but I never called in a bomb threat. Someone did and more than once. We filed out to the baseball fields, everyone baffled at the liberation from drowsy routine. The phone booth: all glass and steel and the light inside the booth had a bluish cast, and the hoaxer spoke through a cloth over the mouthpiece. The hoaxer is hero of the day, has seized the hammer, broken the safety glass and gotten away.

For flying Confederate flags in a Union state
For packing heat inside a white suburban strip mall wonderland
For the fulfillment of bronze belt buckles and fast-food dreams of
management positions
For cutting grass
For emptying out a truck of carnival games and spreading them on
mattress and box springs
For getting a thumping from police

~ August 3, 2015

Gun centerpiece at the reception made it easier to have missed
the wedding.

Leave him in jail, so "to get it over with." His grandma feels bad for
the other inmates because he's so nervous.

~ August 7, 2015

Blogger, critic of ISIS, hacked to death in Bangladesh.

~ August 12, 2015

For solace I spend my days cutting out rooms in the grass. In Queen
Anne's Lace, maybe in Hemlock, I make a home. I walk from room to
room, and when I run out of space I make another one, with gasoline
and a machine, or say the old way with a scythe. A wild turkey with
her nine chicks likes it tall and seedy. She crosses over from the
master suite into the wild: the construction site of future rooms.

Mashed potatoes scooped out like a ball of ice cream. Counting dollars folded in half and wrapped with rubber bands. About five stacks in a plastic bag. He speaks softly to a twenty for over a minute. I write as carefully as he ate, counting words instead of currency. I write slowly as if each word is etched into stone. (Veselka diner, NYC)

Why are we here if not to be makers? About wardrobes for composing, I prefer vintage writing rags, even though I look like a corpse, awakened by a bell, who claws herself out of the grave.

~ *August 19, 2015*
State of Nayarit on the Pacific Coast of Mexico

I soak leafy plants in the sea. Brown pelicans plop into the water, and they are "carved with a jackknife" as Stephen Crane wrote in "The Open Boat." Crabs cling to the rock face. Waves wash in.

~ *August 20, 2015*

Salt & pepper, tequila & weed, beer & wine, milk & coffee, salsa & tortillas, candles & lighter, fruit wash & almond milk, avocados & eggs, razor & toothpaste, groceries in paradise.

Note from beach. Mewling birds who are not quite black, brown breasted, this agitated flock swarms and swarms again. One bird couple inspects the sand as if they were looking for the ruins of their lost home.

Fresh tortillas kept warm in a cooler. Tender and steaming. Tuna, the catch of yesterday but still fresh enough. Grouchy European sells T-shirts emblazed with "Live the Life You Love."

Rain and thunder last night. How many names are there for these
Jurassic Park (the thunder is enormous and wild) claps of car alarm
inducing apocalypse?

Last night's dinner at a no-name jungle cafe: Only seventeen servings
a night of homemade pasta. Laid out on cutting boards. Served
water in a glass with irregular waves. Clear without the blue band at
the mouth. Like drinking from a fruit jar. The water glistening and
glorious in the heat. No fans. Outside at a wooden table. The chairs,
wood frames straight-backed with plastic woven seats. Like sitting
on duct tape and my bare legs are a bit uncomfortable so I shift
throughout. Soccer game next door.

Hippie vans. Both occupied and abandoned on the same street.
California license plates.

Small white herons rest in the treetops in front of my balcony.
Another taller heron, could be same species. Long stick legs and
yellow feet, coexisting with the brown pelicans who are more gray
than brown, more driftwood than earth. Counted forty or so this
morning.

Buzzards ride the sky during the storm, they plummet and then fly
up. Not sure if this is a joy ride or technique for surviving high winds.

Dreamed I took some eggs covered in a blanket to a party and they
hatched during the party. Cute hungry chicks. I frantically search
for a basket and food. Crumbling cake into their mouths, fearing for
the future that I had made. Recognized the root of this dream: at the
market I bought six eggs and they packed them in a baggie instead of
a carton. By the time I got home, I had forgotten about the loose eggs
and dropped the bag onto the counter and broke three. I bought eggs

again the next day, stayed mindful of this delicate package, and made it home with all six intact inside a pink thin baggie.

She says the pharmacy "sells generics of generics." The doctor owns the pharmacy and he keeps regular hours, no charge to see him. The washed instruments lie in a heap on the sink's upper ledge.

Smithsonian writers coming this week for "culture of the Riviera Nayarit" feature. The morning sun fails to shine through the haze.

I'm writing this from the Bay of Banderas; a baby pen for humpbacks in the winter. Not the largest bay and not the Sea of Cortez. That tectonic rift is further north. This is sixty miles of coastline, and the Pacific Ocean is another blue horizon beyond this blue horizon.

Five hundred peso bill, worth a little less than thirty U.S. dollars. Self-portrait of Diego Rivera, in wire-rimmed glasses, and his painting *Nude with Calla Lilies*, don't think it's Frida but rather an earlier lover. The other side, Frida Kahlo's self-portrait with her painting *The Love Embrace of the Universe, the Earth (Mexico), Myself, Diego and Señor Xolotl*, that features Diego as a naked baby cradled by her enormous hands. Their family dog, Señor Xolotl, named for the god who guards the underworld, lies on the arm of Cihuacoatl, the Aztec earth mother who is in turn embraced by the universal mother.

ISIS blew up the ancient city of Palmyra.

On the first full day of this year, I took a walk on the ruins of the Temple Mayor; inside the museum, a cutout of the temples inside of other temples:

Milagros pinned to a shrine
Calcium grins grim
Below the cobblestones
Face to face with volcanic stone
Temples built over temples
Bed of the city lies on a lake
Skulls with spinal cord tails: an offering.
A shaman beat you lightly with branches
It was a blessing, a welcome to this city

At La Casa Azul when the guard left the room I leaned over the velvet
rope to glimpse myself in that mirror but set off an alarm instead.
Like the woman in Amherst caught trying on Emily Dickinson's
white dress, I would have tried too. Could I wear Emily's dress or lie
in Frida's bed? Like typing in a poem that you love and hoping that
poem's glory becomes yours. You're a tourist in local drag, but there
could be a transfer of genius or a blessing if you touch that cloth that
touched them.

The gray pelicans. Mottled like driftwood. Seagulls with forked tails.
Black under the wings. A white bodied one. With bits of red beak.
Beaks outsized, comical to the point of the grotesque. Like a bird, still
wet, that flew out of a Bosch painting.

YouTube diary:
Dead Kids. 1984.
Mind Snatchers. 1974.

~ August 29, 2015

Hermit crabs inhabiting shells smaller than a fingernail.
Dark lizard about a foot long, maybe a pound, hiding inside a
tree trunk.

Heard of using fruit on a stick to lure out iguanas so you can gaze at
their beauty.

Jorge, a marine biologist and fisherman, saw a ridley turtle surface out
in the open ocean. The turtle couldn't breathe because her neck was
wrapped up in part of an anchor line. When Jorge cut her free, the
turtle drank in a large breath and swam away.

Heard rumors that a *Smithsonian* writer covering the culture of
the Nayarit was detained by a discovery of a mass grave of sacrifice
victims under the Temple Major.

Our abode is all white like living inside an eggshell. White on white
and like a broken yolk we muddle the colors.

A graveyard is called a pantheon, and your handmade grave is dug by
your friends.

Flowers and candles cover the grave like a blanket; her portrait is the
headboard. Handful of long stiff wires and rosaries knotted to a tree at
the foot. As he said, "She's beautiful" a candle burning inside a plastic
cup caught the cup on fire.

"We prefer Mexifiles. Not expats" says Joe, a retired pilot and Vietnam
vet who lost his ass in Florida real estate.

~ September 1, 2015

These are the answered prayers of Guadalajara. The supplicants:
a woman with dog gnawing on her leg, man crushed by a boulder,
the sick in bed surrounded by family; Christo on the cross, appears
hovering like a drone in the room.

The shell is a green stone and the legs are silver and extend
across the tops of the other fingers, at first I thought he was wearing
a bird's-head ring. A crowd gathers around him. Caged parakeets.
The methodology: A parakeet picks out paper fortunes from a stack.
With a flourish, the shaman seals the fortunes in a blue envelope for
the recipient to take home.

Squeegee man wiping down a motorcycle for three paper-wrapped
stacks of tortillas.

Mariachi festival: suits with bands of silver buttons, I have followed
some mariachis down the cobblestones, leading wedding parties
that include open pours of tequila and a donkey, and larger-than-life
puppets of a bride and groom.

This is the language. Soft paper, moist. These sounds of water and
fans hushing, coughs hushing us. In the quietude of the market: alone
with a cabinet of bleached ivory hoofs.

                              ~ September 3, 2015

Fishing is a constant. Men fish with a line and hook cast by hand
and wade out in groups to chest-high water and throw out nets.
Women gather snails and mussels from the rocks and wade in the low
gentle surf. In the bay, a father and his son of about six. The father
holds his son horizontally, so that the boy skims the surface of the
water like a great sea turtle swimming towards a fishing boat of other
fathers and sons.

PLAYA DE LOS MUERTOS

The town looks like this: Frida Kahlo in Pancho Villa drag. Strings
of bullets crisscrossed over her chest. Frida of the gift shops, of the
T-shirts. Frida on a surfboard. Frida on a bicycle. Frida on key chains
and plastic market bags. Frida on matchbooks and mirrors. Beads
of plastic Frida forever in the guts of iguanas and coatimundis of
the jungle. Frida forever filling the bellies of breaching whales. In
leatherneck turtles, hatching baby Fridas that swim their plastic
multiple selves out to sea.

Anyone can be buried here, even Canadians and Americans. I don't
know if the cemetery has a name, unless it is simply Los Muertos.

The cemetery is divided by a dirt road, with graves climbing to
the top of the water side, and the other half, vacation homes, built
on hillsides of loose soil, leaf dander, and construction trash. The
living, locals and tourists, cut through on their way to Playa de
los Muertos. Among the locals: mother and daughter team selling
tamales, man peddling donuts from a large tray strapped around his
neck, and another man pushing a wheelbarrow of candy in tropical
colors, up the hill to reach the Beach of the Dead.

The beach lies on the edge of Sayulita, located in the Bay of Banderas,
the Mexican state of Nayarit. This place has a touristy surface, but
underneath is bedrock composed of the families awarded the land
for their service to Pancho Villa. Called the Ejido, these families own
most of the properties due to a pre-Columbian method of governing
and distribution of land. Even though Sayulita was founded in the
early twentieth century, this is an old part of the new world. A few
hours north is Mexcaltitán, an island expanded by landfill in the last

55

century, where the Aztecs believed the world began. It's now a city of canals, to be navigated like Venice.

There are other people, maybe older, the Huichol, who worship peyote and who accept Jesus as a talented shaman, and they live in the nearby Sierra Madre mountains. They sell string paintings based on peyote dreams to the tourists. The men dress in white embellished with bright red elaborate needlework, and the women wear traditional dresses made of layers of black woven wool or cotton. With their children at their feet, they sew and sell small stuffed deer and llamas.

Passing through the graveyard is a harbinger, or warning, on the way to swimming in the bay as the surf can be rough. I am reminded of my mortal coil. How quickly it can be snapped or shuffled off. Some say it's a silver cord that may be glimpsed in trance states and that the cord can expand to cover the universe. You may venture into outer space and then smoothly rewind your soul back into the body with a mere jolt.

Sometimes the oilcloth lifts and the bare legs of a plastic table are exposed. There have been two murders here in recent years, of an American toddler and of a bootleg DVD salesman by mobsters. From the old world: the beating of a gelato shop owner by a rival gelato shop owner, both recent Italian immigrants.

I saw an abyss the night of my father's death. The linoleum parted, and I knew that if I fell off the bed and into that canyon of grief I would never climb out. I knew metaphor was as real as this tabletop, knew that it was a physical place, a site, a geography, a topographical map. I'm reading the anthropologist Michael Taussig's *I Swear I Saw This: Drawings in Fieldwork Notebooks, Namely My Own* where he riffs on making drawings as opposed to taking pictures: how one makes as

opposed to takes an image, drawing upon Barthes and Benjamin and even Burroughs about the notebook as a talisman, a third eye. I heard him speak before on how as the outsider, even a social scientist, one sometimes misunderstands what one sees, however, sometimes like a child, one sees with clarity, without all the baggage of an insider or an adult. In that spirit I took to the cemetery with notebook and pen in hand, to sketch, to see, to misunderstand possibly what I saw.

Some colors and shapes of the cemetery monuments of Los Muertos:
Aqua
Purple
Sky blue
Beige
White with pink trim
Green and yellow
Blue and yellow
Gold framed shrines
Gold plaster and gold painted plastic

Is there a name for these cathedral-shaped monuments? I've seen them before on the Mexican Pacific coast. Like the spires might pierce heaven, each window suggests a room, or say, the window is an opening into the soul. Each has a slab that on the Day of the Dead might become a table.

White with towers
High-rises for candles
Golden doors

Goth tourist couple (living people), tattoos on peeled potato flesh. Boyfriend wearing mutton chops. They inspect the graves with reverence.

Insects, a spider or worm spinning a brown leaf over a grave.
No one lit a candle for the poop off the main path. Fresh-lit candles
in the pre-dawn

Cathedral
Vases
Many lit candles gold frame full front door
Cross-shaped
Window empty of glass
"no estes triste aqui / soy muy feliz"
Three cherubs
Christo
Wreath of plastic flowers encased in plastic

Some movement, laborers emerge from the bushes with concrete
supplies for local building boom.

Months later, looking at the drawings, I recall the difficulty of scale
and of missing some details, a vase or cross, that I inked in after
the first pass. I am more invested in a rude sketch than in a digital
onslaught of photos that may be deleted with a tap.

Maybe this is what I misunderstood or what I saw clearly: these
handmade cemetery monuments show the desire to entomb a loved
one inside a vessel of beauty, of sacred folk architecture, capable of
flight for the rapture: monuments lifting heavenward, despite the
cement and wire frames, and the earthiness of our mortal shells.

IV

Inside *the* Cabin

CAVE

My soul lowered by a thread into a cold lake inside a flooded
mine shaft, five stories down, it felt like a color, not a sensation
of temperature, if it were a color it was chartreuse. I called for a
UFO to show itself and it presented as a plasma screen in the sky.
A sensation like inhabiting a sealed can of wet and plastered grape
leaves, it felt like moonlight inside a paint can. Please keep a lid on
it lest it evaporate, lest it dissolve, like cave paintings destroyed by
human breath. That day I felt a handprint on the inside, it felt like
bruised ribs.

BALD EAGLES

Hot tissue paper in the wind, like a flag was raised from the dirt and
the flag of dirt had powerful feathers. At first it was like ice skating
into a watery hole beneath the dirty flag roosting on serpent's arms.
That feeling lasted all day, my forehead felt useless and hard like a
turquoise ring locked inside a vault.

LOG CABINS

My tongue tastes like lime built up in a cooking pot, and I use a mirror inside an abandoned log cabin to comb my hair, which is as dead and long as antlers; my tears fell like broken glass on the ground that no one bothered to clean up and somehow I arrived in something smaller than a car, and the wooden wheels were like secretly eating in a museum or library.

DRAWING

I began to draw long lines like hoarfrost on a pencil tip and my
fist felt like a hand-grenade, like writing on sandpaper and like
melting my fingerprints on ice. My neighbor's boots are a rough
tongue on carpeting while our doors bounce slightly. It felt like the
time a man offered to tell me a Viking saga, was he speaking in code?
It felt like sleeping under a silver mylar blanket on a bed of pine
needles in the open.

SEX

Afterwards, my thighs and ass felt strong and wild like the dappled horse buttocks inside a Leonora Carrington painting.

RIDING IN A NEW CAR

Riding in a new car is like climbing the devil's tower. The car tastes like luxury coffee and exiting through the passenger side like shopping with credit cards of platinum. We ride and talk trying to catch a glimpse of the devil's nest; it is like returning to a beehive but of human voices, and it stings to be near language.

NOISE

Cerulean white or like library books on loan. I felt unable to fit my
noises into a handkerchief. Withheld sneezing and avoided catnip.
Like an arm slipped and bounced down on spinning vinyl, like forks
and knifes cause cosmic disturbances. The silence of that hour hung
in the air, a glass ornament.

WESTERN LANDSCAPES

My neighbor's voice spoke about the surface management of a
common mammal and the place names tasted bittersweet; it seemed
as if a map engraved itself on my back, and every visible rut became
a ballad of local disasters, and monuments erupted from the memory
of my spleen or other organ meats. There was a house, occupied by
white settlers, this house was made of wood and hewn from a
single log.

FLYING OVER SNOW

Near a small city, the snow became brown and fear wove a weighted blanket of blood inside my mouth.

A FOREST OF BERLIN

A bouquet of twigs and moss and a hard orange burst of flowers. Everyone in the forest wore black clothing, like a uniform of darkness.

Bear-lin, or Bear's den, or Burr-lin, and the bear at the door.

Toy trucks and other smalls hidden under a shirt. Passing window view: Reichstag replica in porcelain and full of a wintery liquor; everyone sleeps during the day, clothing is tight and purposeful. Each street tells a sexy love story or a grim fairy tale. In Berlin everyone knows the little walking man, his hat shaped like a soft skillet and everyone keeps a suitcase of tiny toiletries stashed. In Berlin, the ends of your hair fade into turquoise. Bread is made of nuts and seeds and cakes are rhubarb or apricot. The forest is thick with witches and all your hard wires smoke like the flame from a fat candle.

I sat outside a cafe with a blanket on my lap doing heavy eating, I woke in a city of bears that smelled of dairy farts, of meat and cheese; I woke in a city where even the toys smoked, a plastic bear smoked a plastic cigarette, and a toy bird, filled with red liquid, dipped its beak into a water glass over and over for my amusement. That city turned my own face into something hairy and soft. And these smells followed me home from the airport.

While in this city of bears, I heard of a maiden who lived in a guard tower, even though she was not a Checkpoint Charlie. Every evening she stroked her hair with a boar bristle brush; the guard dogs below, German shepherds, were serious, large and wet, and their ears pointed forward.

But a bear wanted the maiden's tower (prime real estate). Bears are persistent and clever, and this bear had heard that a poem, the words in the right combination, could spring open the heavy door reinforced with Bronze Age rebar.

So the bear said ". . . hmmm" and the maiden said, "Yes, like that." The door fell open like an unhinged jaw of a giant and she fled with German shepherds to find the human whose words were stolen by the bear. After roaming for years, she wondered if the bear had eaten the poet.

Time is a long corridor of dogs and towers.

In later chapters, she found herself locked inside a house of hair and a castle of friendly pleasures. She was held captive in a dungeon of lust hidden on a vast estate where there were instruments molded from a Poe story, in which a device meant a tool worked by hand to break the halos of medieval lambs.

INSIDE THE CABIN

Coffee cups
stirrer sticks
napkins and cookies
on the tray top
satellite TV
office in the air

rearrange the drinking vessels
compose a still life
below gray rocks and ice

Icelandic air smells of curdled milk or codfish

Greenland's snow creased
like complex elephant skin
outside the airship, −54° c.

sea waves   stitched quilt batting

blue of the online flight tracker
a flat blue wash around currents and land mass
over Newfoundland and Greenland
the deep blue hours of our bodies over bodies of water

Deepest blue on the screen is the Labrador Sea, a marginal sea,
an alleyway between Baffin Island and Greenland. Labrador is not to
labor, not to work one's way across the sea or not a laboratory for
experimenting in remote territories. Rather the name of a dog
species who roam the Canadian arm that reaches toward
Greenland

Pushing face against the portal to look for human habitation, for
buildings and traffic. Seatmates, a young couple, maybe lovers; I had
the sense that once on land they would split up, and perhaps they
had never seen snow

Will myself to think of ice floes, not of Basquiat's doorway of
layered graffiti and posters, big lips pasted over the door and do
not think of those who pause there, to absorb paint / heroin / fame
clouds like traces, of a portrait of David Bowie on the rails of a
gate on Bond Street and on the subway posters of the 6 Train

Icelandic Air, an airborne Viking ship "Jarðhraði 907 km/h" over the
eastern green edge of Greenland. I study the screen and see the globe
is blue, green and white with edges of light surrounding land masses

The airplane icon trail is a solid line of where we've been and the
future is a perforated line that remains to be neatly folded on the
table's edge and torn

bitten edges of continental plates wet with plant life,
all is a fissure
crevice
gap
slip
portal
plummet
abyss

73

Stokur steam rising from flat earth of

> lava fields, scoured,
> porous rock.
> behind a chain, muddy
> hole belches
> god's guts

Condensation on the plastic window, make a streak or line and
seek a source of water nearby

I come from the Americas
from a valley of mound builders,
from artifacts that are mine and not mine

A mammal of the Americas,
hunting morels / firewood / berries

Or is it a matter of gods? The kind you make, the kind you
worship, the kind you appease

Gods built from a fiery void or the gods who crawl out of the
earth

I am a European, but I come from the Americas
Casting rune stones from Row 23, Seat F
for safe passage over the North Atlantic

No one passes without an offering
Passport & change of clothes
Wedding band, dental implants & surgical hardware

The Inuit are the only ones who can see the mother of the North
sea

Maybe the world's tree is a trade route,
pulp of the world's tree is a paper cup
sitting on the tray of Row 23, Seat F

Amass an architecture of freebies:
plastics, more durable than gods

In flight over belief systems
The names of the gods change
And cannot be murdered, only transformed
Even slaughtered into bits, an eyeball becomes the sun, or a toe
becomes a volcano   severed fingers become
lakes, falling tears become waterfalls

Buried sitting up in a boat, and the boat is the long house, and the
long house is the hall, and the entry to other worlds is through the
keyhole

Sorceress's white lead-painted face, robed in a cloak of blue cloth,
wearing pouches of animal organs and herbs
and her belly is filled with pellets of fat and ash

Skins, gutted but for skull and hoofs,
stretched over a frame of sticks
Given to a body of water

We in Row 23 are perfect for delivering a tribute
dropping coins, flesh, roots and herbs,
effigies for shadow selves

Buried inside a long boat, filled with magic amulets, gall bladder,
spleens, heart and gizzards of animals, and with a horse's bridled
beloved head

I have not arrived on a strange sledge
pulled by dogs on an ice floe
Not chasing a monster that I made
Not chatting with deckhands at sea

seats upright
devices off
prepare for landing
on an island
still being born

V

Mortal Beauty

MORTAL BEAUTY

Angel with a bright red suitcase came to the door

We walked the streets of Catskill

We walked alleys and ice cream parlors

I saw my future in a jar so I dashed it to the floor

I saw small pieces of wood ground into the dirt

The walls throbbed from the roots up and asked,
"Are you the one who made the angel?"

The angel with the bright red suitcase never complained about the beauty of mortals

One day the angel opened the suitcase

The suitcase contained the seeds of all living things

Puppies and babies, fruits and nuts, and seeds as small as dots of dust

When the angel opened the suitcase the seeds of all living things
burst out like a brood of cicadas

With only days to live

Acknowledgments

Many of these poems appeared in the following journals and
websites: *American Poetry Review*, *Arabella*, *Bomb*, *Brooklyn Rail*,
Chant de la Siréne the Journal, *Dispatches Ecopoetics*, *Global Poemic*,
Hurricane Review, *Metambesen*, *Ping Pong*, *Prospect*, *Poetry Salzburg*,
St. Rocco for the Dispossessed, *The Doris*, and *Wonderlust*. Other poems
appeared in collaborations with the following visual artists and in
galleries—Joseph Carey: *20 Poems for 20 Paintings*; Emily Harvey
Foundation Masque Show; and Max Warsh: *Momentarily*.

Thank you to Tanis Hofmann and Jorge Pantoja Tapia for
generously sharing their knowledge of the Nayarit coast of Mexico.
And to Erica Hunt who suggested the title "Journal of Places."

Thank you to the *UnWalled* show with Corinne May Botz and
Elana Herzog and the Fahrenheit 451 House, and to Richard O'Russa
and Soho Press for letter pressing "Mortal Beauty."

A hearty thank-you to Sarah Cohen and poets Marcella Durand,
Jennifer Firestone, Tonya Foster, Erica Hunt, Rachel Levitsky, Helen
Mitsios, Baruch November, Karen Weiser, Evie Shockley, and Simone
White and to the visual artists who rearranged my senses through
their work and conversation: Trine Bumiller, Santiago Cohen, Elana
Herzog, Heidi Howard, Robert McDaniel, Portia Munson, and
Alexis Myre.

Deep bows to Kristin Prevallet for insight and order and to
Eleni Sikelianos for her suggestion on how to work within the frame
of an hour.

Thank you for providing space, time and community: Emily
Harvey Foundation, Gloucester Writers Center, Robert Rauschenberg
Foundation Residency, and Ucross Artist Residency.

About the Author

BRENDA COULTAS is a contemporary American poet. She is the author of the collections *The Tatters* (Wesleyan University Press, 2014), *The Marvelous Bones of Time* (Coffee House Press, 2007), and *A Handmade Museum* (Coffee House Press, 2003). She teaches at Touro College and has served as faculty in Naropa University's Summer Writing Program. She lives in New York City.